Ants at Camp

Written by **Kristin Anthian**
Illustrated by **QBS Learning**

Fast phonics

Before reading this book, ask the student to practise saying the sounds (phonemes) and reading the new words used in the book. Try to make it as speedy and as fun as possible.

Read the tricky high frequency words

The student can't sound out these words at the moment, but they need to know them because they are commonly used.

all   the   as

to   is   her

Tip: Encourage the student to sound out any sounds they know in these words, and you can provide them with the irregular or tricky part.

Say the sounds

This book introduces blending adjacent consonants: **VCC** and **CVCC** words. This includes the suffix **-s**.

ff   ll   ss   x   ck   w

Tip: Remember to say the pure sounds. For example, 'sssss' and 'nnnnn'. If you need a reminder, watch the *Snappy Sounds* videos.

Snappy words

Point at a word randomly and have the student read the word. The student will need to sound out the word and blend the sounds to read the word. For example: 'a–nnn–t, ant'.

an	help	gust
ant	just	pals
end	went	hits
camp	tent	ants
best	lost	sets
wind	next	pegs

Quick vocabulary check

The underlined words may not be familiar to the student. Check their understanding before you start to read the book.

Liz went to camp.

All her best pals went as well.

Jack

Kim

Liz

It is the best camp.

Kim and Jack help Liz
put up the tent
next to the pond.

Liz just lost
all the tent pegs.

Next, a big gust of wind hits the tent.

The tent is a mess.

An ant nest!

Get off the tent, ants!

Liz went to fix the tent.

But the tent is
just next to an ant nest.

All the pals sip hot milk.

The ants get hot milk as well.

The sun sets.

Off to bed!

It is the best end to camp.

Comprehension questions

Well done!

Let's talk about the story together
Ask the student:
- Why did the tent become a mess? What happened?
- How did the pegs get lost?
- What does 'the sun sets' mean?
- Why was Kim thinking 'mmm'?

Snappy words
Ask the student to read these words as quickly as they can.

gust	wind	hits	ant
nest	sets	milk	end

Fluency
Can the student read the story again and improve on the last time?

Have fun!